W9-AAI-391

MAKERSPACES™

GETTING THE MOST OUT OF MAKERSPACES TO CREATE WITH
3-D PRINTERS

NICKI PETER PETRIKOWSKI

ROSEN
PUBLISHING

Published in 2015 by The Rosen Publishing Group, Inc.
29 East 21st Street, New York, NY 10010

Library of Congress Cataloging-in-Publication Data

Petrikowski, Nicki Peter.
Getting the most out of makerspaces to create with 3-D
printers/Nicki Peter Petrikowski.
    pages cm.—(Makerspaces)
Audience: Grades 5–8.
Includes bibliographical references and index.
ISBN 978-1-4777-8602-4 (library bound)—ISBN 978-1-
4777-7813-5 (pbk.)—ISBN 978-1-4777-7814-2 (6-pack)
1. Three-dimensional printing—Juvenile literature. I. Title.
TS171.95.P47 2015
621.9'88—dc 3

                                                    2014001079

Manufactured in the United States of America

CONTENTS

The technology of 3-D printing will revolutionize the way things are made, allowing virtually anyone in the world to make any object.

W hat if you could make anything you wanted anytime you wanted? What sounds like a dream is gradually becoming reality. A new do-it-yourself trend called the maker movement is making this dream possible. Among the many innovative computer-controlled tools that are used in this movement, the most astounding is the 3-D printer. Much like a regular printer can print out a picture or text file, these machines can turn a digital 3-D model into a real, tangible object, and they are becoming more and more widespread. All over the world, makerspaces (places where people can gather, share ideas, learn, and use tools like 3-D printers to let their dreams become reality) are opening their doors.

This type of printing is a way to turn a digital file into a physical object. Something designed on a computer is turned into a solid, tangible form through an additive manufacturing process. Rather than taking away from the material to form an object (which would be a subtractive process, like wood carving), the printer lays down layer upon layer of the printed object. This is an economical process. It takes only the precise amount of material that is needed to form the desired object without any waste. It can be quite magical to see something take shape as if from nothing.

What use could an individual have for a 3-D printer? The possibilities are endless. If you can imagine it, you can print it (although there are some physical limitations to the process). People have used 3-D printers to make art, jewelry, toys, and gaming pieces, but also replacement parts for household items such as lamps and remote controls. This can be extremely practical, especially if the parts in question are no longer produced by the company the items came from.

Many 3-D printing enthusiasts share their designs online. Some even go on to market their products, which the newly accessible technology allowed them to make without having to invest huge amounts of money into more traditional means of production. Not everybody can afford to build their own factory, but cheap 3-D printers offer great opportunities for aspiring entrepreneurs of modest means.

In this book, you will find information about the maker movement, its origins, and its values, as well as learn where to find a makerspace near you and what you can expect to find there. One thing you are likely to find is a 3-D printer, and this book will tell you what they are capable of, how they work, and how you can use them to create your own projects.

The maker movement has received a lot of media attention recently, and some even say that it could revolutionize the way our economy works. So who are these people, what is their goal, and what effect can the movement have on society?

CHAPTER ONE
A Revolution in the Making

Given the name, it is hardly a surprise that members of the maker movement first and foremost want to make things. What they want to make and how they go about it differs from maker to maker. It doesn't even have to be the wish to make something specific—maybe it is a general urge to create. This urge to create something can be seen as the defining characteristic of members of the maker movement.

Humans have, of course, been making things for thousands of years. Yet, in recent history, the number of people working at jobs where they actually create something tangible has decreased, and a lot of manufacturing has been outsourced to places where labor is cheap. Many people now work at a computer all day, creating websites, software, or other forms of digital content. This is important work, but it is work that does not produce physical objects. There has been a similar trend in schools, where shop class, which was once required, has become an elective. Students are taught to work with computers rather than how to make things with their own hands reflecting the changes in the job market. But producing something you can touch, smell, or even taste gives a unique sense of accomplishment, which has led people to take up making, the creating of real things, as a hobby.

Making things is not revolutionary in any way. People have always made things in their free time. Hobbyists and tinkerers have had their workshops in their garages or basements to work on gadgets and inventions. For the most part, these were solitary activities that were maybe shared with a few local friends. With the Internet, though, that changed, as people could easily find others from all over the world with whom could share an interest, talk about their ideas, and develop them together.

The web has allowed for collaboration that was simply impossible before. Digital designs can easily be shared in online communities and improved in cooperation. New tools make it far easier to turn these digital designs into physical objects. The key here is computer numerical control (CNC) machine tools that are controlled precisely by a computer and can produce what has been designed on the computer, using computer-aided design (CAD) software.

PRINTING IN 3-D

One of the tools that has been met with a lot of interest is the 3-D printer, a technology that has been around for decades but has only recently become affordable for private individuals. These tools play into the strengths of the generations that have grown up using computers. They open up opportunities that did not exist before, as they allow the production of things on a small scale that previously would have required huge investments in manufacturing plants. And if you want more copies of your designs than you can easily make yourself, you can send the designs to a service provider with larger production capabilities and pay it to make your product for you.

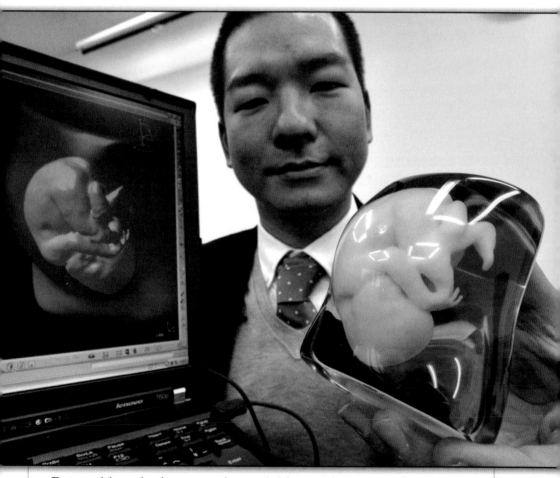

Being able to look at an unborn child is made even more amazing with a 3-D printed model of the fetus.

A GATHERING OF MAKERS

A Maker Faire is a gathering of makers who show their creative projects and share ideas. Maker Media cemented its position as one of the cornerstones of the maker movement by holding Maker Faires, billed as "the greatest show and tell in the world."

The first Maker Faire was held in San Mateo, California, in 2006 and became a runaway success. The big events produced by Maker Media, especially those in New York and the San Francisco Bay Area, can have hundreds of makers presenting arts, crafts, and science projects and tens of thousands of curious attendees. Smaller events organized by local communities are known as Mini Maker Faires. Hundreds of these celebrations of the maker movement take place all over the world, and they are a great way to learn, meet people, and have fun. To find a Maker Faire near you, visit the Maker Faire website.

THE (R)EVOLUTION IN MANUFACTURING

The Internet hasn't only revolutionized the way designs are made and shared. It has also had a huge impact on how products are sold. A web store can reach countless more potential customers than a local store ever could, making niche products that are made only in relatively small numbers commercially viable. Millions of makers are selling their products on sites such as Quirky and Etsy and on crowdfunding sites such as Kickstarter and Indiegogo. On crowdfunding sites, people can pledge money for projects they want to see get made, allowing entrepreneurs to finance their endeavors without having to go through a bank as long as they find enough backers.

These new tools both in production and marketing allow more products to enter the market; these products can be more customized because they don't have to be made and sold in huge quantities. The means of production don't lie in the hands of a small number of companies anymore. They are open to more people than ever before, who can create (almost) anything with a mouse click.

Allowing people to present their projects and collect funding from others who want to see them become reality, crowdfunding sites like Kickstarter (www.kickstarter.com) have opened up new possibilities for makers.

CHAPTER TWO

THE MAKER ETHOS

Despite what has been said about financing and selling in the previous chapter, makers aren't usually in it for the money. Unlike companies that have the declared goal of making a profit, makers normally see their making as a hobby. While some makers go on to found their own companies, some of which have even become very successful, finding a new way of earning their living is not the reason why people start out making. However, it can be a by-product. So if money is not the driving force, what is it that makes makers make?

"EXPERIMENTAL PLAY"

In an article titled *The Maker Mindset,* Dale Dougherty, founder of *Make* magazine, called the origin of the maker movement "experimental play." Makers are fueled by a childlike curiosity that is sated through playful experimentation (without forgetting safety, of course). They want to know how things work—and how to make them better. They don't resign to being restricted by what they are able to buy, which may not fit their needs as well as it could. So instead of just being passive consumers, they choose to be active creators, making customized things that fit their needs better and hold greater value to them than mass-market products.

A 3-D printer can turn an idea that has been captured by digital means into physical reality.

Makers believe that if you can imagine something, you can make it. Even if you don't know how yet, you can learn. And learning does not need to take the form of formal education. Making is often more hands-on, which means learning by doing. Hands-on learning requires a willingness to fail and not get discouraged. Rather, you learn from any mistakes and make something better.

Do It Together

Do-it-yourself (DIY) projects have been around for a long time. The DIY market, and especially home improvement, is a billion-dollar industry. Doing them together isn't new, either, with their initiators commonly recruiting the (more or less willing) help of family members and friends.

While home improvement requires the physical presence of those working on the project, that is often not the case with maker projects, as these start as digital designs. These can be shared on the Internet and allow project starters to get help from people outside of their immediate social circle, or even the continent they live on. People from all over the world who share an interest can easily come together on the Internet, exchange ideas, and collaborate on a project.

The maker movement embraces this, and the spirit of doing things together has carried over from the digital world into the real world. The cooperative culture is apparent when makers meet, for example in a makerspace, where generally they will eagerly share ideas and knowledge as well as tools. As Mark Hatch noted in *Maker Movement Manifesto*, "The sharing philosophy gives a makerspace its magic" and turns it into a community.

THE PERSISTENT-TINKERING MENTALITY

David Lang's endeavor to become a maker after losing his job was documented in a column for *Make* magazine and a book he financed through Kickstarter. He defines the maker mentality as the "persistent-tinkering mentality," a "combination of unshakeable optimism, unlimited opportunity, and never-ending satisfaction." You don't have to be perfect at what you are trying to do. In fact, you can hardly be perfect at something you haven't tried yet in practice. But you have to keep on trying, continuously improve upon what you have done, accept challenges, and do your best to overcome them.

SHARING ACCOMPLISHMENTS

One thing that helps with that is that you don't need to do it alone, as makers like to share. They take pride in what they are making and like to present it to others. Being able to show your accomplishments gives great satisfaction, but it's not just about bragging rights. The accomplishments and the experience of others are a fantastic source of information, and generally makers are willing to share their knowledge. And sharing information about a project you are working on can lead to other people offering insights of their own that may result in further improvements.

Makers often take their sharing to another level by giving away what they have made. That doesn't simply mean that they are giving an object they have created, such as a nameplate made with a laser cutter or a 3-D printed vase, as a gift to friends or family members.

They often are giving away their designs for others to use and alter so that everybody can benefit from them, not just the people who worked on them.

Such a level of generosity would hardly be possible if money was makers' first concern, but it doesn't necessarily prevent them from making money, either. These 3-D printers are a good example of how makers can make money. The designs of many printers on the market today can be traced back to the RepRap project, an Internet-based collaboration to create a 3-D printer. The designs for this machine are freely available for anybody. In theory, everybody could use them to build one.

For many people, though, convenience is more important than saving a bit of money. They would rather buy an already-built machine than build one themselves, opening up a market for those willing to meet the demand. Also, since the design was made by people volunteering their time and expertise rather than by paid developers, a product that emerges from the maker movement can often be offered at a cheaper price than one that was developed by a company in a more traditional way. Giving away your designs means, of course, that others can bring products based on them to market and compete with you. However, competition and the innovation it brings are seen as positive things.

Shown at the Consumer Electronics Show in Las Vegas, Nevada, these colorful 3-D printed bunnies are just a playful example of what this technology is capable of.

Mark Hatch declared in his *Maker Movement Manifesto*: "The best hope for improving the world is us, and we are responsible for making a better future." Its open and optimistic atmosphere and its ideals of sharing and giving have made the maker movement more than just a collection of people who make things.

CHAPTER THREE

OPENING UP A NEW SPACE

What is a makerspace? As the name implies, it is a space where people can make things, but it isn't just any space that provides tools. While people may make things in their garages or kitchens, these are generally not makerspaces. Rather than being private and secluded, makerspaces are open for a community to use and interact in.

FROM HACKERS TO MAKERS

The idea of having a communal space for people to work in together on their hobby derives from the hackerspaces started in the 1990s in Europe, particularly in Germany. Local clubs associated with the Chaos Computer Club, Europe's largest association of hackers, set up spaces to collaborate on their computer projects. One of the earliest and best-known hackerspaces is c-base, which was founded in Berlin by seventeen people in 1995 and exists to this day with upwards of five hundred members. The maker movement was also active in the United States during this time and there were some early community creative spaces, such as the Crucible, which opened in Oakland, California, in 1999.

In 2007, after seeing these spaces in Germany and being inspired by them, hackers from the United States started setting up spaces of their own, such as NYC Resistor and Noisebridge in San Francisco. As computer numerical controlled (CNC) machine tools such as laser cutters, milling machines, and 3-D

Gatherings of the Chaos Computer Club, which can indeed seem chaotic, were one inspiration for the creation of makerspaces.

printers became more affordable, they found their way into these spaces. This opened up new possibilities as to what could be made there.

The term "makerspace" was coined by Dale Dougherty of Maker Media, who figured it had a more open and positive ring to it than "hackerspace". The term "hacker" is often used mean "computer criminal," although in a broader sense it is a name for a computer enthusiast exploring the limits of hardware and software. The term "makerspace" became popular after Dougherty started the website Makerspace.com in 2011, with resources on how to set up a community center with tools.

"Hackerspace" and "makerspace" are often used interchangeably. However, the *Makerspace Playbook* says that makerspaces "focus primarily on learning and education, whereas hackerspaces often focus on hobbyists who make to have fun and relax, or who use the space as an incubator for their emerging small business." That is not always the case, and places calling themselves "hackerspaces" usually offer classes as well. Yet they may have a stronger focus on computers and electronics than makerspaces. They may also offer more traditional tools.

Regardless of classes, though, these spaces tend to be great for learning. Not only do they encourage experimenting, but the people there are generally eager to share their knowledge and are willing to give some tips or lend a hand.

FAB LABS AND TECHSHOP

There are two franchises of makerspaces that came into being before the first independent makerspaces opened up in the United States in 2007. The Crucible opened in Oakland, California, in 1999. Fab labs, short for fabrication laboratories, are part of a network started by Neil Gershenfeld from the Center for Bits and Atoms at the Massachusetts Institute of Technology in 2005. He was inspired by a course titled "How

How to Find a Makerspace in Your Area

Makerspaces are becoming more and more common. Schools and universities, especially, are at the forefront of this movement. They are beginning to offer their students access to the machines and education necessary to make. Many public libraries, as places of community engagement, are also opening makerspaces of their own to offer an additional service to their patrons. If your school or library does not have a makerspace, it might be worth asking about the possibility of opening one so that the decision makers are aware that there exists an interest.

A directory of existing makerspaces is featured on Makerspace.com, where you can also get a copy of the *Makerspace Playbook*, a guide on how to set up such a place. The most complete listing online can be found at Hackerspaces.org, where a map shows hundreds of locations all around the world, in addition to a list of planned makerspaces that have not opened their doors yet. Even if there is no location in your immediate area, the site is a good resource for getting in touch with other makers and learning about upcoming events and other developments.

to Make (Almost) Anything," first held at MIT in 2004. The fab labs are meant to allow just that. Unlike independent makerspaces, they must adhere to specific requirements as to what tools they offer.

TechShop, while offering similar services to a maker-space, is different. Unlike the community-based hacker- and

TechShop locations, as well as many makerspaces, offer the tools that people normally don't have easy access to so that they can work on their projects.

makerspaces, TechShop locations across the United States operate for profit. The company, started in 2006, grants access to its spaces and equipment for a monthly or annual fee and offers fee-based classes.

WHAT TO EXPECT AT A MAKERSPACE

It is difficult to know what to expect from a makerspace, as each one is unique. For independent makerspaces, there is no definite list of requirements other than that they provide tools, space, and an open atmosphere for people to get creative and make.

The equipment can range from hammers and screwdrivers to power tools such as drills, bandsaws, and sewing machines. Equipment can also include computer-controlled tools such as laser cutters and 3-D printers. The latter are somewhat popular in makerspaces, though, and are often in high demand. They also exemplify what is great about makerspaces: they allow the sharing of resources that people wouldn't otherwise have easy access to.

While the prices of these tools may have come down considerably in recent years, they are not at the stage (yet) where they are as affordable and widespread as more traditional tools. So it is great to have a space where you can experiment with them and see what they can do without having to invest a lot of money. By lowering the barrier of entry, makerspaces enable more people to make and share what they are making.

CHAPTER FOUR

New Dimensions in Printing

It may seem like something out of a science fiction movie, but 3-D printing is not a new technology, although many people are only now taking notice. The first 3-D printer was created in 1984 by Charles W. Hull, who cofounded 3-D Systems in 1986, and the technology has been used by big companies for decades.

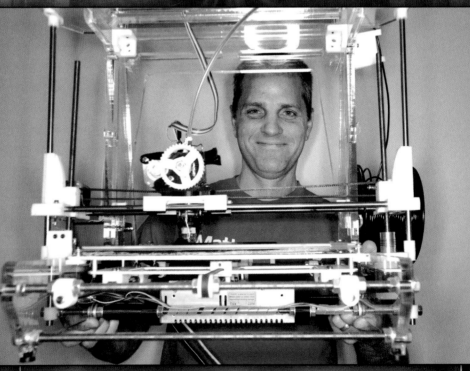

Cost and size used to restrict 3-D printers to being used by big companies, but there are now models available that a regular person can afford—and carry around.

Since 3-D printers were prohibitively expensive, with prices going into the tens if not hundreds of thousands of dollars, few people had access to them. This has changed in recent years. These printers have become so affordable that they are finding their way into private households. Some people expect them to be as widespread in just a few years as regular two-dimensional printers are today. But not only will the number of users grow, the number of different uses for this technology will increase as well.

AMAZING WAYS TO USE 3-D PRINTING

Different technologies are employed in 3-D printers. The first 3-D printer created by Charles W. Hull, using a process called stereolithography (SLA), in which layers of a special material are cured by a beam of ultraviolet light. Selective laser sintering (SLS) uses lasers to fuse a powder made out of metal or plastic, which forms the printed object.

The most common technology in 3-D printers aimed at the consumer market and most likely to be encountered at makerspaces is fused filament fabrication (FFF), also called fused deposition modeling (FDM). These printers use plastic filament as a material, which is heated and forced through a nozzle to form the layers of the printed object, which fuse together. The workings of fused filament fabrication will be looked at in greater detail in the next chapter.

A Look into the Future

In the television series *Star Trek*, when Captain Picard wants his favorite beverage, he simply steps up to the replicator machine and says, "Tea. Earl Grey. Hot." This machine from science fiction that can produce anything in the blink of an eye by rearranging subatomic particles is far removed from our 3-D printers, which generally use only one or two different materials and can take hours to print an object. Although our technology may never actually reach that level of the replicator machine, it will certainly approach it. Progress will make the printers faster and allow for more detailed prints and the use of different materials. This will make the printing of more complex items possible.

It is only a question of time until there is a 3-D printer in space. NASA is already using them on Earth, and it is not hard to imagine how helpful it would be to have such a machine on the International Space Station. In an environment where you can't just step out and go to a store, the means to produce something you need can be invaluable.

Even more exciting, though, is the potential of 3-D printers on Earth. While we do have the option to go to a store, what if we didn't have to? What if we could just print almost everything we wanted in our own homes? The impact that 3-D printers could have on our economy and our entire way of living are going to be huge, and there are those who expect this technology to bring about a new industrial revolution.

In the manufacturing industry, 3-D printers have been used for rapid prototyping. For a manufacturer of cars or planes, it is easier, faster, and cheaper to design concept parts or the prototype of a model on a computer and print it out rather than building one through traditional means. This is especially true because this technology has made it easy to make adjustments to the design and simply print a new version.

Printing Human Organs

The possibilities of 3-D printing are endless. As fantastic as having such a device in one's household may be, the use of 3-D printers in medicine are truly astounding. Already they are used to produce cheap mechanical prosthetics. Since the designs are easily modified, this is particularly beneficial for children who outgrow their prosthetics, as a fitting replacement can simply be printed. Doctors can print models of a patient's organs before operating to plan the procedure and make it safer. There are even experiments using live cells as material, which could render animal testing obsolete and make it possible to print transplantable organs.

Printing Actual Houses

Another humanitarian use of 3-D printers is being done on a much larger scale: the printing of entire houses. Using concrete as a material, the printers being developed currently could build a house in a matter of hours rather than weeks, making housing more affordable due to the reduced labor costs. Rather than erecting emergency shelter, it might be

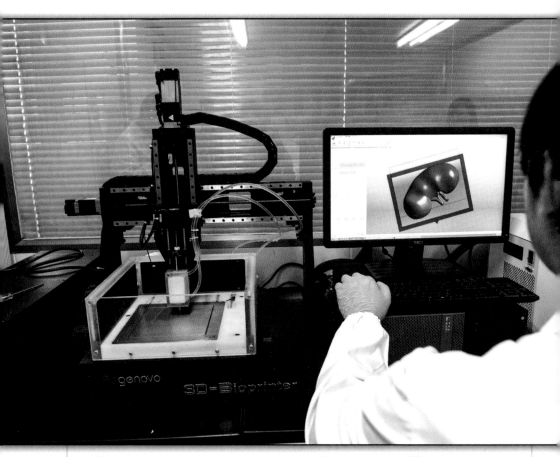

Already machines exist that can print human tissue. The prospects for future use of this technology in medical treatments are immense.

possible in a few years to immediately print new homes for those who have lost theirs to a natural disaster.

Already 3-D printing is changing the world in ways both small and big, and there seems little this technology cannot do. It is getting faster, cheaper, and better at a staggering rate and will continue to do so.

CHAPTER FIVE

A LOOK INSIDE A 3-D PRINTER

Before using a 3-D printer, it is a good idea to get an understanding of how it works, to grasp its capabilities and limitations. Since printers at makerspaces most likely use fused filament fabrication (FFF) technology, it will be explained here.

THE FASCINATION OF FUSED FILAMENT FABRICATION

An FFF-based printer uses thermoplastic filament, basically a thin string of plastic that is heated to reach a semiliquid state, which allows it to fuse, to fabricate the desired object. At the heart of such a printer is the extruder and hot end, which work together to extrude molten plastic. The extruder pushes the plastic filament forward. The filament usually has a diameter of 3 or 1.75 millimeters and is provided in the form of a spool. The hot end has a heated chamber to melt the plastic, which is then extruded through a nozzle to form the layers of the object being printed. The plastic squirted from the nozzle is not safe to touch, as it is extremely hot (between 340° and 430°F [171° and 221°C]), depending on the plastic being used). The size of the nozzle that the molten filament is forced through determines the level of detail the printer can achieve. This opening is generally only between 0.35mm and 0.5mm in diameter.

Producing a miniature chair of such intricate design by more traditional means would be difficult indeed. A 3-D printer effortlessly builds it layer by layer.

The extruder pushes the plastic forward, and the hot end squirts the layers of the object being printed onto the build platform or printbed. This platform is often heated, which prevents the cooling plastic from warping, so it should not be touched, either, as long as the printer is working.

FROM TWO DIMENSIONS TO THREE

The head of an inkjet printer has to move in only two directions, from left to right (along the X axis) and from top to bottom (along the Y axis), to print on a sheet of paper. A 3-D printer requires movement in a third direction, along the Z axis, so it can produce a three-dimensional object.

Different printer models accomplish this in different ways, for example, by having the extruder move along the X and Y axes and the printbed lowering itself on the Z axis away from the extruder. No matter which parts move in which direction, all three axes of the Cartesian coordinate system are required for positioning the extruder. It is important that the movement is stable so that the printing can be done with the necessary precision.

THE 3-D PRINTER FRAME

To help with stability, 3-D printers have a rigid frame, which can be made from different materials. Some manufacturers, especially those that offer self-assembly kits, favor wooden structures. These can be made with laser cutting machines that are also often available at makerspaces. However, there are models with metal or plastic frames available as well. Some of these structures even have handles so that the printer can be carried like a suitcase for easier transport.

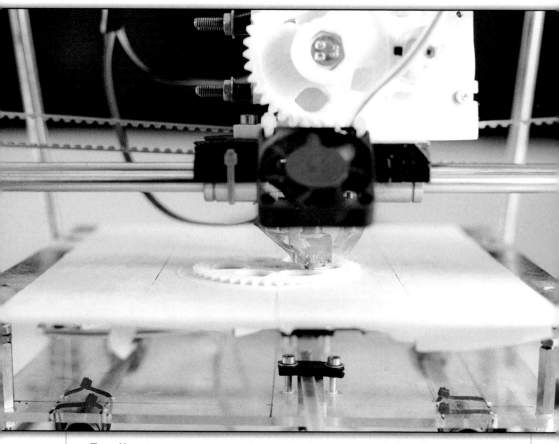

By allowing movement along the three axes of the Cartesian coordinate system, a 3-D printer can create almost any shape.

Almost all printers have an open case or a viewing window, though, so it is possible to watch the printing process.

One thing you have to consider when planning to print an object is the printer's build volume. Just as a regular printer has its limits in how big a sheet of paper it can print on, a 3-D printer can only fabricate objects up to a certain size determined by the size of its printbed and the height of its Z axis.

Materials Used for 3-D Printing

There are different materials available to use with FFF printers, and their differences go beyond the thickness and color of the filament. Two kinds of plastic are particularly popular: acrylonitrile butadiene styrene (ABS) and polylactic acid (PLA).

ABS is a versatile, impact-resistant plastic that is used to produce toys like LEGOs. When it is heated, it gives off toxic fumes, so proper ventilation is required when working with this material. It also has the downside of shrinking slightly when it cools, which can cause the printed object to warp, but a heated build platform can prevent that.

PLA is a popular option for 3-D printing as this biodegradable plastic is less prone to warping and does not require a heated printbed. It produces less toxic fumes, it extrudes at a lower temperature, and it is stronger and more rigid—but also more brittle—than ABS. Depending on the circumstances, both materials can have their uses.

Another printable filament is polyvinyl alcohol (PVA), essentially the same as PVA glue. Since PVA dissolves in water, some printers use a second print head to build support structures for the object being printed in plastic, which can be easily removed after the printing is complete. This al-

lows for more complex objects with angles that otherwise could not be achieved, as they would droop. Generally, a 3-D printer cannot produce an overhang of more than 45° without some sort of support structure.

While these are the most commonly used materials, there are others with different properties that people are experimenting with, like wood fiber filament or nylon and even conductive filament, which allows the printing of functioning electronics.

These limits differ considerably from model to model so it is best to find out beforehand if the printer at your makerspace only allows for a small object or a more massive one. Even if the printer cannot handle the dimensions you had in mind, it might be an option to print the design in more than one part and assemble the parts afterward.

MAKING THE NECESSARY PREPARATIONS

The 3-D printer is not at the same stage yet as a regular printer, which you can simply take out of the box, connect to your computer, and use to print right away. They require a bit more work to set up and calibrate properly. The build platform needs to be level, the movement along the three axes needs to be smooth, the filament spool needs to be installed properly, the heat settings need to be set correctly, and you need to be sure that the extruder is not jammed. It's always better to double-check rather than risk a distorted print job. At a makerspace, there should be somebody present overseeing the use of the machines who can help with the proper preparations.

CHAPTER SIX

MAKERS ON THE MARKET

The market for 3-D printers aimed at and priced for private individuals is still relatively young. However, there are already numerous options available, and the number of competing printers is only bound to get bigger. In one edition of *Make: Ultimate Guide to 3D Printing*, sixteen different machines were reviewed; in the next edition, that number increased to twenty-three new printers from just as many different manufacturers. Hardly a week seems to go by without a new model being announced or presented on crowdfunding platforms like Kickstarter or Indiegogo.

INFINITE CHOICES

In a field that is evolving and expanding as quickly as 3-D printers, it is rare to find a constant. The technology is changing at a rapid pace, and so are the models available to buy. One constant in this young market, although not unchanged, is MakerBot. Founded in 2009 by Bre Pettis, Zack Smith, and Adam Mayer, MakerBot is one of the most established and popular brands of 3-D printers and therefore one commonly found in makerspaces.

The RepRap project, an Internet-based collaboration, gave people instructions on how they could build their own 3-D printer. Doing so from scratch was a challenge, as it wasn't easy

In only a few short years, MakerBot has grown from a small company selling kits to a big business employing more than one hundred people to assemble its 3-D printers.

to find all the necessary components. So MakerBot put together a kit called Cupcake CNC that could be assembled in a matter of hours and started selling it in March 2009. Although it incorporated many lessons learned from the RepRap project, MakerBot did not try to offer a machine that could replicate itself. Instead of this somewhat philosophical goal, it focused on providing a kit for hobbyists to experiment with.

Early on, its designs were freely available. You did not have to buy the kit from MakerBot to build your own Cupcake, provided you could find all the parts on your own. In September 2010, a new and improved kit, the Thing-O-Matic, was introduced that featured a heated build platform and a larger build volume, followed by the Replicator in January 2012. Unlike the previous models, this one was not sold as a kit but as an assembled printer, making it easier still for people to start printing. When the model was replaced only nine months later by the Replicator 2, MakerBot stopped making its designs freely available.

The RepRap Project

In early 2004, Adrian Bowyer, then a lecturer in the Mechanical Engineering Department at the University of Bath in England, wrote a short article titled "Wealth Without Money," wherein he outlined the impact a self-copying rapid-prototyping machine would have. According to Bowyer, such a machine would allow for the wealth it produces to grow exponentially, just as the number of these machines in existence would grow exponentially. Each new copy would be able to produce more copies of the machine itself, and the more copies of the machines there were, the more things they could produce as well. This, in turn, would mean that these machines, which cost only as much as the materials used to produce them plus the cost to assemble them, would be cheap enough for almost everybody to have one.

Everybody owning such a machine would then be able to produce not only copies of the machine itself to give to others, but also a wide array of other things that they could either design themselves or find designs for on the Internet. Suddenly the masses would have access to the means of production, which before were restricted to a few people with a lot of money (because the more traditional means of production—as you would see in a factory—require great investments).

To try and put this theory into practice, the RepRap project was started in 2005 with the goal of designing a replicating rapid prototyper, a self-copying 3-D printer, the plans for which everybody had access to and was allowed to modify under a free license. Many of those who went on to produce and market their own 3-D printers started out as members of the RepRap community.

While the RepRap project has so far not reached the goal of creating a machine that can make a complete copy of itself—the RepRap currently can produce 50 percent of its own parts—it has succeeded in making the means of rapid prototyping available to more people at an affordable price.

MAKERBOT WARS

From that point on, if you wanted to have a MakerBot, you had to buy it from MakerBot, a step that was met with criticism from the open-source community that MakerBot had arisen from. That did not stand in the way of its success, though. In one edition of *Make: Ultimate Guide to 3D Printing*, it declared: "For ease of use and excellent print quality

The Printrbot Simple, here presented by Brook Drum, the founder of Printrbot, is an interesting option for those looking to buy a 3-D printer, due to its low price.

right out of the box, the MakerBot Replicator 2 is still the printer to beat in the prosumer market." With a price point upward of $2,000. it is one of the more expensive alternatives on the market, too.

On June 19, 2013, MakerBot merged with Stratasys in exchange for shares worth $403 million, a figure that shows how much value is placed on the future of this technology. Stratasys, a company that has been building industry-level 3-D printers for decades, wanted to enter the consumer market to stay competitive with its chief rival, 3-D Systems, who had started offering affordable printers with its model called Cube.

OTHER MANUFACTURERS

Other manufacturers include Ultimaker, Felix Robotics, Formlabs, Deezmaker, OpenBeam USA, and too many others to list them all. However, one model that deserves special mention is the Printrbot Simple from Printrbot. *Make* declared it "the perfect machine in terms of cost, ease of use, and results." As this printer costs only $299 for a kit or $399 for an assembled machine, it makes up for its small build volume with a very affordable price.

Another printer with a comparable price is the Buccaneer from Pirate3D, which raised more than $1.4 million on Kickstarter. At less than half the price of other models available, these will no doubt find their way into many homes and makerspaces.

CHAPTER SEVEN

FROM BITS TO THINGS

Before 3-D printers can turn digital files into physical objects, these digital files have to be created. To turn an idea into a 3-D model, you need computer-aided design (CAD) software. Then, to turn the 3-D model into instructions that allow a 3-D printer to print it out, you need a slicing engine.

CREATING FOR FREE IN 3-D

Just like a graphics program such as MS Paint or GIMP allows you to draw two-dimensional pictures that you can print out on an inkjet or laser printer, a CAD program makes it possible to create three-dimensional models that can be printed with a 3-D printer. For many years, CAD software was the domain of engineers and architects. The programs were far too expensive and complicated for anybody who did not do so professionally. Recently CAD applications have been created that are both easier to use and afford; some of them are even available for free.

One of the most prominent makers of CAD software is Autodesk. In addition to a variety of programs that the company sells, it also offers 123D, a suite of software you can download for free. In addition to a design program that lets you build your own 3-D models, aptly named 123D Design, it also includes 123D Catch, a program that turns a smartphone into a 3-D scanner.

Parametric Modeling

Parametric modeling is a different approach to CAD. Rather than drawing an object, it is formed by defining its parameters (hence the name), the most significant of which are its dimensions. This may be less intuitive. Also, learning the necessary programming language may be more work. In return, though, this method allows for more precise results than CAD software with a graphical interface.

Shapesmith is a browser-based program for parametric 3-D modeling that is quick, easy to use, and available free of charge, as are the downloadable FreeCAD and OpenSCAD.

First released in early 2011, Tinkercad, a browser-based tool for 3-D modeling, also became a popular option. After its makers announced that they would close down Tinkercad, it was purchased by Autodesk. The basic functions of this tool are available for free, but commercial use requires a monthly fee.

Another option is SketchUp, formerly developed by Google and now owned by Trimble Navigation. While there is a commercial version available in SketchUp Pro, the basic version of the software, called SketchUp Make, is free for personal use. Although its makers claim SketchUp to be "the

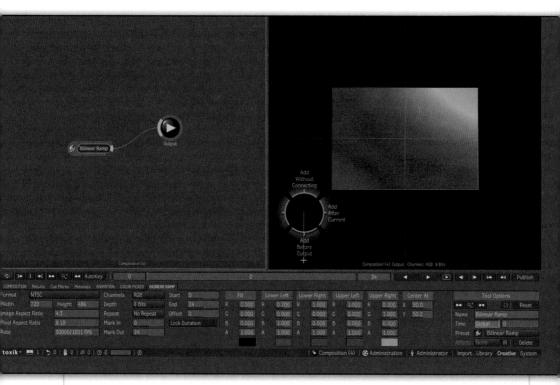

3-D modeling software may be complicated and difficult to learn, but is also very powerful and allows you to do amazing things.

easiest way to draw in 3-D," it has a fairly high learning curve owing perhaps to the fact that originally SketchUp was created for design professionals.

Blender is a 3-D animation suite best suited for more advanced users. Aside from 3-D modeling, its features include animation, rendering, motion tracking, and video editing, and Blender has been used in the creation of movies and computer games. While the learning curve is steep, Blender probably

offers the most features of all the CAD software packages available for free.

All of these programs have different strengths, and it is worth the effort to try out more than one to see which best suits your needs.

SketchUp, which was bought by Google in 2006 and sold to Trimble Navigation in 2012, is one of the most popular 3-D modeling programs available as freeware.

3-D SCANNING

The perfect complement to a 3-D printer is a 3-D scanner. These scanners create digital 3-D models from real-life objects, which can then be reproduced by a printer. They are also becoming more affordable and faster. AIO Robotics even offers a machine that combines a 3-D printer and a 3-D scanner. Its model Zeus is a 3-D copying machine.

Yet it isn't necessary to have a dedicated device for scanning. There are several apps available to turn a smartphone or tablet computer into a 3-D scanner. You can use the device's camera to view the object of interest from different angles. It is then turned into a 3-D model. An added upside is that this can be done almost anywhere and without being restricted to scanning objects of a certain size.

CUTTING YOUR 3-D MODEL INTO PIECES

Once you have your finished 3-D model, the second piece of software needed is a slicing engine. As the 3-D printer produces an object layer by layer, a slicing engine slices a 3-D model into layers and sets a path on how the printer's nozzle has to move and how much material it has to squirt out to build each of these layers before moving on to the next one. This information, called the G-code, is then transferred to the printer so that it can begin its work.

Analyzing the shape of a physical object, a 3-D scanner collects data that can be used to make copies of the scanned object with a 3-D printer.

There are several slicers available, including Skeinforge, SFACT, ReplicatorG, KISSlicer, and Slic3r. These programs allow you to define settings such as the resolution and the height of the layers being printed. The smaller the layer height, the more layers will be needed to print an object. More layers mean the transition from layer to layer will be less visible in the finished object. However, the print job will take longer.

Depending on the shape, it might be possible to print an object as completely hollow, but that would make it fragile. On the other hand, printing an object as a complete solid is often not desirable either, as that uses up more material than actually necessary and is more time consuming. You can determine a fill pattern, often formed similarly to a honeycomb, to give the printed object enough stability without wasting material.

47

CHAPTER EIGHT

SOME COOL PROJECTS

The beauty of 3-D printing is that you can create almost anything you can think of, be it a replacement for a button missing on a favorite jacket, a personalized mug, an art project, or a piece of jewelry you always dreamed of but had no idea how to produce. The possible uses for a 3-D printer are as unique as their users, and everybody will have their own ideas on what they might want to print. If, however, you need some inspiration or just want to get an impression of what is possible with this technology, there are lots of interesting projects to be found on the Internet.

DOWNLOADABLE REALITY

Probably the biggest collection of downloadable 3-D models can be found on Thingiverse, a site founded in 2008 by Zack Smith, cofounder of MakerBot. Although the site is owned by MakerBot, you don't have to have one of its printers to use it.

On the site, a large community shares more than one hundred thousand 3-D models, which users can "like" and comment on just as one does on a social networking site. Unique features to Thingiverse are the "I Made One" tab, where users who have downloaded a design can post pictures to show off their printed object. Users also have the ability to "Remix It," that is, post a modified version of the original

A New World of Intellectual Property

While a 3-D printer may enable you to print just about anything, that doesn't mean that it is legal to do so. Many 3-D models that can be found online are shared under a free license, which means that anybody can use and even alter them. However, that does not mean intellectual property laws can be ignored and that anything can be copied. Copyrights, trademarks, and patents protect many commercial objects, and infringing them is illegal, which needs to be kept in mind. Undoubtedly, the mass distribution of 3-D printing technology will bring with it many legal questions.

File sharing has had an effect on the film and music industries (although not nearly as disastrous as they feared). Similarly, it can be expected that the sharing of three-dimensional designs that people can print out in their homes will have an effect on many manufacturers and force them to adjust their business models.

Action figures, lamps, vases, tools, a tablet computer stand in the form of octopus arms, and even printable shoes—you can find pretty much anything on Thingiverse.

Other sites are Shapeways and Trimble 3D Warehouse. Shapeways offers a 3-D parts database with free files that it

Unlike more traditional means of production, 3-D printing makes it easy to produce personalized items, like action figures that look like you.

has tested and will, so it claims, "print for sure," which is not always guaranteed with user-generated content. The Trimble 3D Warehouse is a library of designs to accompany the SketchUp CAD software. Autodesk also offers a library of models made with its Autodesk 123D Design program.

Other sites that feature collections of 3-D models include GrabCAD, 3D ContentCentral, Inventables, TurboSquid, and CGTrader—some that are free for download, as well as models that have to be bought.

3-D printing can be used for an incredibly wide variety of things, creating your own fancy footwear being only one creative example.

WHERE TO BEGIN

Having a world of options open to you can be a little intimidating and make it hard to choose. As always when trying something new, it is best to start with something simple so as not to get discouraged.

While a project with many parts may be extraordinary, it is also complex and has little to no margin for error. A 3-D printed name tag, personalized pencil holder, or

PRINTING SERVICES

If you want to have an object printed but don't have access to a 3-D printer locally, there are service providers to help you out. Companies such as Shapeways, i.materialise, and Ponoko will take your digital designs, turn them into physical objects, and ship them to you. Unlike makerspaces, which likely have only one or two printers available, these service providers can manage larger print runs. They can also offer prints in different materials, from plastic to ceramic and various metals.

These services do have a price, of course, and generally it will be cheaper—and faster, since you don't have to wait for your item to be shipped—to print at a makerspace. However, the professionalism these companies offer can be worth it.

An alternative to the professional companies is 3D Hubs, a website where every person owning a 3-D printer can register and offer his or her machine up for rent to local makers.

cell phone case may be a more basic project, but it is still impressive and fascinating to watch it being printed, not to mention practical. Objects printed with a 3-D printer make great gifts, too. Once you have successfully printed your first projects and are familiar with how the process works, you can move on to more challenging endeavors.

acrylonitrile butadiene styrene (ABS) A thermoplastic often used as material for 3-D printers.

build platform This platform or bed is the surface onto which a 3-D printer prints an object.

build volume The maximum size of an object that a 3-D printer can produce.

computer-aided design (CAD) Software that is used to design three-dimensional objects.

crowdfunding A way of financing a project by collecting money from a number of individuals who want to see the project get made, usually via the Internet.

extruder The part of a 3-D printer that pushes plastic filament through the hot end.

fused deposition modeling (FDM) Another name for fused filament fabrication (FFF).

fused filament fabrication (FFF) The technology used by the most widespread 3-D printers, which uses plastic filament to form the layers of the printed object.

G-code The code transmitted from a PC to a 3-D printer to give it instructions on how to print.

hacker A person who is proficient with computer hardware and software and likes to experiment with them. Some, but not all, hackers use their proficiency for illegal activities.

hot end The part of a 3-D printer that heats plastic filament and squirts it onto the build platform to make an object.

layer height As 3-D printers print objects in successive layers, the layer height determines the resolution of the print, or how visible the different layers are on the finished object.

makerspace A space where people can come together to make objects, sharing a collection of tools. They are sometimes also called hackerspaces or hacker labs.

polylactic acid (PLA) A biodegradable thermoplastic made from starch, used as filament for 3-D printers.

polyvinyl alcohol (PVA) A water-soluble filament that is often used as support material in 3-D printing.

RepRap Short for replicating rapid prototyper, this machine envisioned by Adrian Bowyer in 2004 was the spiritual ancestor of many 3-D printers now on the market.

selective laser sintering (SLS) A technology used in 3-D printers that uses a laser to fuse small particles into layers.

slicer A program to turn CAD files into G-code by cutting a three-dimensional design into slices that a 3-D printer prints out as layers.

stereolithography (SLA) The first method of 3-D printing, in which objects are formed by material being cured through ultraviolet light.

3-D printer A printer that can turn digital designs into physical objects using different materials, such as plastic or metal, that are printed out in layers.

Maker Education Initiative
1001 42nd Street, Suite 230
Oakland, CA 94608
(651) 263-9979
Website: http://www.makered.org
The Maker Education Initiative, a project of the Tides
Center, a registered nonprofit public charity, has the mission
"to create more opportunities for young people to develop
confidence, creativity, and spark an interest in science, technology, engineering, math, the arts, and learning as a whole
through making."

MakerKids
2241 Dundas Street West
Toronto, ON M6R 1X6
Canada
(416) 534-3848, ext. 127
Website: http://www.makerkids.ca
Makerkids is a nonprofit makerspace with lots of programs
for young makers.

Maker Media
1005 Gravenstein Highway North
Sebastopol, CA 95472
Website: http://makermedia.com
Maker Media, publisher of *Make* magazine and organizer of
the Maker Faires, is one of the forerunners of the worldwide
maker movement.

NYC Resistor
87 3rd Avenue
Brooklyn, NY 11217
(347) 586-9270
Website: http://www.nycresistor.com
NYC Resistor is probably the most famous makerspace in the United States. Some of its founding members went on to start MakerBot Industries.

Thingiverse
MakerBot Industries, LLC
One MetroTech Center, 21st Floor
Brooklyn, NY 11201
Website: http://www.thingiverse.com
Thingiverse, powered by MakerBot Industries, one of the most prominent producers of 3-D printers, is the world's biggest 3-D printing community where people share their designs.

WEBSITES

Due to the changing nature of Internet links, Rosen Publishing has developed an online list of websites related to the subject of this book. This site is updated regularly. Please use this link to access the list:

http://www.rosenlinks.com/MAKER/Print

Au, Jesse Harrington. *3-D CAD with Autodesk 123D: Designing for 3-D Printing, Laser Cutting, and Personal Fabrication.* Sebastopol, CA: O'Reilly, 2014.

Baichtal, John. *Hack This: 24 Incredible Hackerspace Projects from the DIY Movement.* Indianapolis, IN: Que Publishing, 2012.

Gershenfeld, Neil. *Fab: The Coming Revolution on Your Desktop—From Personal Computers to Personal Fabrication.* New York, NY: Basic Books, 2005.

Griffin, Matthew. *Design and Modeling for 3D Printing.* Sebastopol, CA: O'Reilly, 2014.

Hood-Daniel, Patrick. *Printing in Plastic: Build Your Own 3-D Printer.* New York, NY: Apress, 2011.

Hoskins, Stephen. *3-D Printing for Artists, Designers and Makers: Technology Crossing Art and Industry.* London, England: Bloomsbury Visual Arts, 2014.

Kelly, James Floyd. *3-D Printing: Build Your Own 3-D Printer and Print Your Own 3-D Objects.* Indianapolis, IN: Que Publishing, 2013.

Kemp, Adam. *The Makerspace Workbench.* Sebastopol, CA: O'Reilly, 2013.

Lipson, Hod, and Melba Kurman. *Fabricated: The New World of 3-D Printing.* Hoboken, NJ: John Wiley & Sons, 2013.

Martinez, Sylvia, and Gary Stager. *Invent to Learn: Making, Tinkering, and Engineering in the Classroom.* Torrance, CA: Constructing Modern Knowledge Press, 2013.

McEwen, Adrian, and Hakim Cassimally. *Designing the Internet of Things.* Hoboken, NJ: John Wiley & Sons, 2013.

O'Neill, Terence, and Josh Williams. *3-D Printing*. Ann Arbor, MI: Cherry Lake Publishing, 2013.

Pettis, Bre, Anne Kaziunas France, and Jay Shergill. *Getting Started with MakerBot*. Sebastopol, CA: O'Reilly, 2013.

Preddy, Leslie. *School Library Makerspaces: Grades 6-12*. Santa Barbara, CA: Libraries Unlimited, 2013.

Roslund, Samantha, and Emily Puckett Rodgers. *Makerspaces*. Ann Arbor, MI: Cherry Lake Publishing, 2014.

Sheppard, Kimberly. *3-D Printing—Unabridged Guide*. Dayboro, Australia: Emereo Publishing, 2012.

Singh, Sandeep. *Beginning Google SketchUp for 3-D Printing*. New York, NY: Apress, 2010.

Thornburg, David. *From the Campfire to the Holodeck: Creating Engaging and Powerful 21st Century Learning Environments*. San Francisco, CA: Jossey-Bass, 2014.

Anderson, Chris. *Makers: The New Industrial Revolution*. New York, NY: Cornerstone Digital, 2012.

Apell, Henri. *Faszination 3D-Drucker. Erste Einblicke in Eine Revolutionierende Technik*. Kindle ed., 2013.

Bagley, Caitlin A. "What Is a Makerspace? Creativity in the Library." ALA TechSource, December 20, 2012. Retrieved December 2, 2013 (http://www.alatechsource.org/blog/2012/12/what-is-a-makerspace-creativity-in-the-library.html).

Bowyer, Adrian: "Wealth Without Money." February 2, 2004. Retrieved December 2, 2013 (http://reprap.org/wiki/BackgroundPage).

Budmen, Isaac, and Anthony Rotolo. *The Book on 3-D Printing*. Seattle, WA: CreateSpace, 2013.

Cavalcanti, Gui. "Is It a Hackerspace, Makerspace, TechShop, or FabLab?" *Make*, May 22, 2013. Retrieved December 2, 2013 (http://makezine.com/2013/05/22/the-difference-between-hackerspaces-makerspaces-techshops-and-fablabs).

Desai, Deven R., and Gerard N. Magliocca. "Patents, Meet Napster: 3-D Printing and the Digitization of Things." October 12, 2013. Retrieved December 6, 2013 (http://papers.ssrn.com/sol3/papers.cfm?abstract_id=2338067).

Dougherty, Dale: *The Maker Mindset*. Retrieved December 16, 2013 (http://llk.media.mit.edu/courses/readings/maker-mindset.pdf).

Dougherty, Dale, et al. *Make: Ultimate Guide to 3D Printing 2014*. Sebastopol, CA: Maker Media, 2013.

Evans, Brian. *Practical 3-D Printers: The Science and Art of 3-D Printing*, Berkely, CA: Apress, 2012.

Fastermann, Petra. *Die Macher der Dritten Industriellen Revolution: Das Maker Movement*. Norderstedt, Germany: BoD, 2013.

Good, Travis. "What Is 'Making'?" *Make*, January 28, 2013. Retrieved December 9, 2013. (http://makezine.com/2013/01/28/what-is-making).

Gustin, Sam. *How the 'Maker' Movement Plans to Transform the U.S. Economy. Time*, October 1, 2012. Retrieved December 9, 2013 (http://business.time.com/2012/10/01/how-the-maker-movement-plans-to-transform-the-u-s-economy).

Hatch, Mark. *The Maker Movement Manifesto: Rules for Innovation in the New World of Crafters, Hackers, and Tinkerers.* New York, NY: Mcgraw-Hill Professional, 2013.

Hlubinka, Michelle, et al. *The Makerspace Playbook*. Maker Media, 2013. Retrieved December 2, 2013 (http://makerspace.com/wp-content/uploads/2013/02/MakerspacePlaybook-Feb2013.pdf).

Hornick, John. "Some Thoughts on Copyright and 3-D Printing." 3-D Printing Industry, September 13, 2013. Retrieved December 6, 2013 (http://3-Dprintingindustry.com/2013/09/13/some-thoughts-on-copyright-and-3-D-printing).

Kemp, Adrian. "Skill Badge Guide: 3-D Printing." Adafruit Learning System. Retrieved December 3, 2013 (http://learn.adafruit.com/skill-badge-guide-3-D-printing).

Lang, David. *Zero to Maker: Learn (Just Enough) to Make (Just About) Anything*. Sebastopol, CA: Maker Media, 2013.

Mearian, Lucas. "3-D Printing Techniques Will Be Used to Construct Buildings, Here and in Outer Space." *Computerworld*, September 18, 2013. Retrieved December 2, 2013 (http://www.computerworld.com/s/article/9242482/3-D_printing_techniques_will_be_used_to_construct_buildings_here_and_in_outer_space_).

Walter-Herrmann, Julia, and Corinne Büching (eds). *FabLab. of Machines, Makers and Inventors*. Bielefeld, Germany: Verlag, 2013.

ABOUT THE AUTHOR

Dr. Nicki Peter Petrikowski is a literary scholar, as well as an editor, author, and translator. As an avid collector of miniature figures, he is looking forward to expanding his collection with 3-D printed models.

PHOTO CREDITS

Cover, p. 1 © iStockphoto.com/Sebastien_B; p. 4–5, 47, 51 Britta Pedersen/picture-alliance/dpa/AP Images; pp. 7, 12, 18, 24, 29, 36, 42, 48 © iStockphoto.com/Chesky_W; p. 9 Yoshikazu Tsuno/AFP/Getty Images; p. 11 © iStockphoto.com/DanielBendjy; p. 13 Keystone/Gaetan Bally/Redux; p. 17 Justin Sullivan/Getty Images; p. 19 Patrick Lux/Getty Images; pp. 22, 40 © AP Images; p. 24 (inset) © Eugene Garcia/The Orange County Register/ZUMA Press; p. 28 © Xu Yu/Xinhua/ZUMA Press; p. 30 Imaginechina via AP Images; p. 32 Tomas Mikula/Shutterstock.com; p. 37 Bloomberg/Getty Images; p. 44 PRNewsFoto/Autodesk, Inc./AP Images; p. 45 Ethan Miller/Getty Images; p. 50 Rex Features via AP Images; cover and interior page design elements © iStockphoto.com/Samarskaya (cover wires), © iStockphoto.com/klenger (interior wires), © iStockphoto.com/A-Digit (circuit board design), © iStockphoto.com/Steven van Soldt (metal plate), © iStockphoto.com/Storman (background pp. 4–5).

Designer: Nelson Sá; Editor: Nicholas Croce;
Photo Researcher: Karen Huang